INTRODUCTION

Welcome to the *Hal Leonard Greek Bouzouki Method*! The Greek bouzouki is a popular instrume[...] is a lot of fun to play. Its bright and lively sound is the essence of Greek music and a big part of many other Mediterranean and Balkan styles. The bouzouki is often used to accompany the melodies of singers or other instrumentalists, but it also really shines as a lead instrument. This method will teach you to play melodies, strum chords, and even do a little of both at the same time.

ABOUT THE VIDEO EXAMPLES

All of the accompanying videos for this book can be accessed online for streaming or download. Visit *www.halleonard.com/ mylibrary* and enter the code found on page 1 of this book. Video examples are noted throughout the book with the icon seen here: ▶

ABOUT THE GREEK BOUZOUKI

The national instrument of modern Greece, the bouzouki descended from instruments that were brought by immigrants from Turkey in the early 1900s. Its rounded back, made of strips of wood (or **staves**), is similar to that of its close relatives, the Greek *lauto* and Italian *mandola*. The original bouzoukis had three pairs (or **courses**) of strings, but these days the *tetrachordo* or four-course bouzouki is the choice of 'zoukists everywhere.

GREEK BOUZOUKI ANATOMY

headstock —

tuning keys

nut

frets

neck

fretboard

strings

bridge

staves

tailpiece

PLAYING POSITION

 VIDEO 1 *To access all the accompanying videos, simply visit* **www.halleonard.com/mylibrary** *and enter the code from page 1 of this book.*

The Greek bouzouki's rounded back and long neck make it a challenge to hold comfortably, but the proper playing position will keep you and the instrument balanced.

- Sit on a knee-high, armless chair or stool.

- Keep your left foot on the ground but raise your right foot slightly (2–4 inches) with a small footstool or footrest.

- Rest the body of the bouzouki on your lap so that the neck is angled slightly upward (30 degrees from horizontal).

If the body slips off your lap, try putting a thin rubber or leather pad on your right thigh, then resting the instrument on it. (A piece of non-slip shelf lining works well for this.) Alternately, if your bouzouki has strap buttons, you could use a thin guitar strap.

TUNING

When tuning the bouzouki, you adjust the **pitch** (highness or lowness) of each string by turning its corresponding tuning key. Loosening the string lowers the pitch, and tightening the string raises the pitch.

The bouzouki's strings are numbered 1 to 4. Although the instrument has a total of eight strings, each pair, or **course**, is tuned to the same pitch and played at the same time. Therefore, each course is counted as one unit. String course 1, the thinnest pair, is the D course; the fourth pair is the C course, the thickest and lowest pair.

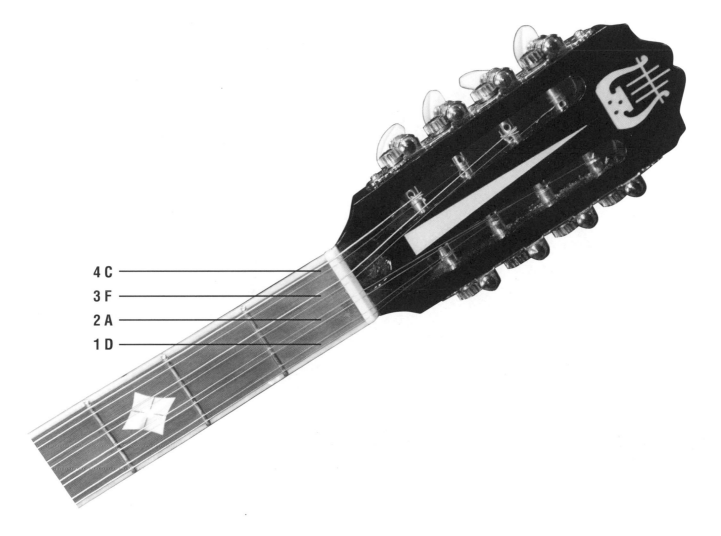

VIDEO 2

The accompanying video plays a set of notes you can use to tune your bouzouki by ear. We start with the first course—the highest, D. Match both of the strings in your bouzouki's first course to this note. Next is the second course, A, then the third course, F, and finally the fourth course, C. Play one string at a time when tuning.

You will notice that the F and C courses have high (thin) and low (thick) strings. These are **octaves**, two versions of the same note in different registers.

ELECTRONIC TUNERS

An electronic tuner can help you get in tune quickly, but it is also important to train your ears to hear when a string is out of tune. If you use an electronic tuner, be sure to pay attention to the sound of the strings when they are in tune. Each pair will sound without vibrations when they are in tune with each other.

THE RIGHT HAND

Note: if you are a left-handed player, reverse the right- and left-hand instructions.

Developing good technique on both hands right away is very important; bad habits can lead to sloppy playing and repetitive stress injuries! See the photos for proper playing position.

HOLDING THE PICK

Hold the pick between your thumb and index finger so that the pointed end is at a 90-degree angle to the thumb. Hold firmly but not too tightly, keeping the thumb straight, and move your wrist when you strike the strings.

HAND POSITION

Hold your hand over the strings near the bridge. Your lower palm could touch the strings behind the bridge very lightly, but don't push on the strings—it will mute the sound and make the notes sound out of tune!

THE LEFT HAND

The left-hand fingers change the notes you're playing by pressing on the strings (or **fretting**). If you've never played a fretted stringed instrument before, your fingers might get a little sore at first. Don't worry; the more you play, the easier it will get!

Depending on what you are playing, your left hand will often sit in a guitar-style position, with the thumb on the back of the neck. This usually works best for chords.

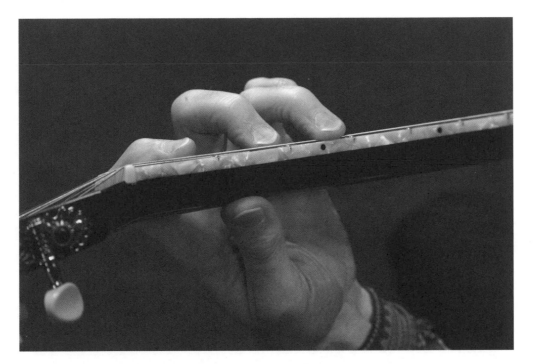

Sometimes you will need to hold your hand in a mandolin-style hand position, with your thumb loosely wrapped around the neck. This position works well when playing single notes.

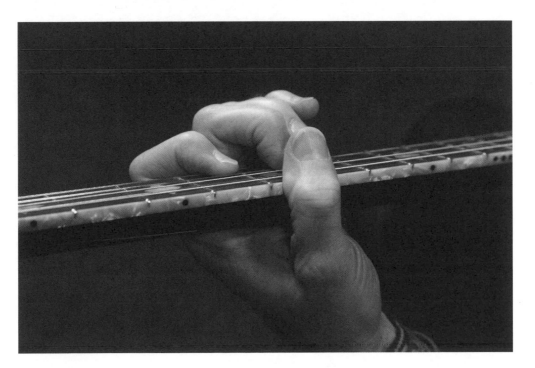

In either case, the thumb needs to be relaxed. Be sure not to grip or pinch the neck too tightly, or you will pay the price with sore hands and sloppy technique!

MUSIC NOTATION

Music is written in **notes** on a **staff**. The staff has five lines and four spaces between the lines. Where a note is written on the staff determines its pitch (highness or lowness).

STAFF

At the beginning of the staff is a **clef sign**. Bouzouki music is written in the **treble clef**.

TREBLE CLEF

Each line and space of the staff has a letter name. The **lines** are (from bottom to top) **E–G–B–D–F** ("**E**very **G**ood **B**oy **D**oes **F**ine").

LINES

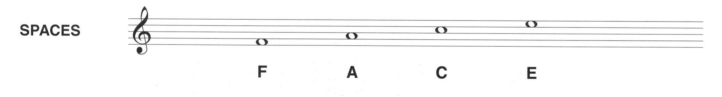

E   G   B   D   F

The spaces are (from bottom to top) **F–A–C–E** ("face").

SPACES

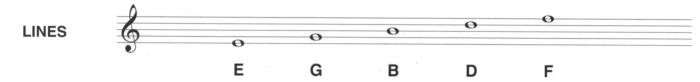

F   A   C   E

Notes are written above and below the staff with lines called **ledger lines**.

LEDGER LINES

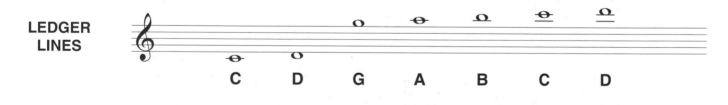

C   D   G   A   B   C   D

The staff is divided into several parts by **bar lines**. The space between two bar lines is called a **measure** (also known as a "bar"). At the end of a piece of music a **double bar** is placed on the staff.

BAR LINES

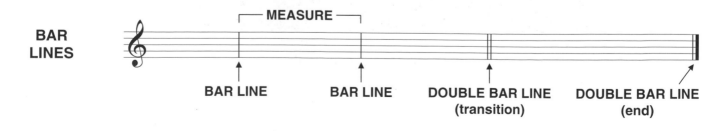

┌— MEASURE —┐

↑   ↑   ↑   ↗
BAR LINE   BAR LINE   DOUBLE BAR LINE   DOUBLE BAR LINE
                                          (transition)   (end)

TABLATURE

Tablature ("tab") is an ancient method of notating music for fretted instruments. In tab, the strings of the instrument are represented by horizontal lines. The frets are shown by numbers written on those lines.

The lowest course of strings (C) is represented by the bottom line:

Numbers on the tab lines present the frets where your left-hand fingers press the strings. (A zero means that string is played **open**, or unfretted.)

In this example, three different notes on three different courses are played one after the other. The first course (D) is played open, the second course (A) is played on fret 3, and the fourth course (C) is played at the fifth fret.

Two or more notes played at the same time—called a **chord**—is indicated in tab with stacked notes.

Tablature will show you where to play the notes, but you still need to look at the notation to know the note names and their **values** (quarter note, eighth note, etc.). Continue reading and working through the book to learn more about note values.

TIME SIGNATURES

The **time signature** shows two things: the number on top shows us the number of beats in a measure, and the number on the bottom shows us what type of note gets one of those beats. If you tap your foot steadily, count "1, 2, 3, 4," and repeat, you are establishing a **4/4** time signature.

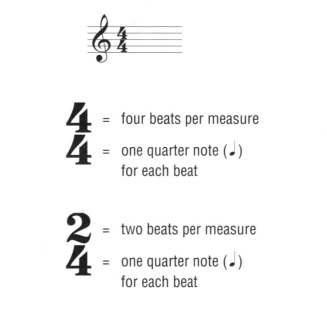

OPEN STRINGS

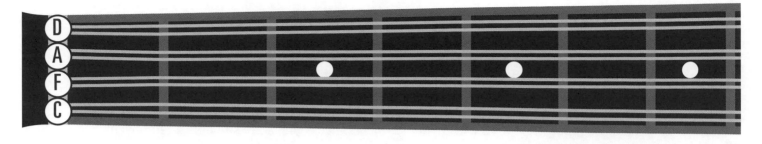

On the following open-string examples, start out slowly and pick each course of strings evenly. Start on the lowest course of strings, C.

Pick downward (toward the ground), using **downstrokes**, as shown by this symbol: ⊓

The following examples are in 4/4 time. Remember, in this time signature, there are four **quarter notes** in each measure, and each note takes up one beat or tap of the foot.

Pick the open C four times (once for each beat), then move to the F, A, and D strings.

VIDEO 3

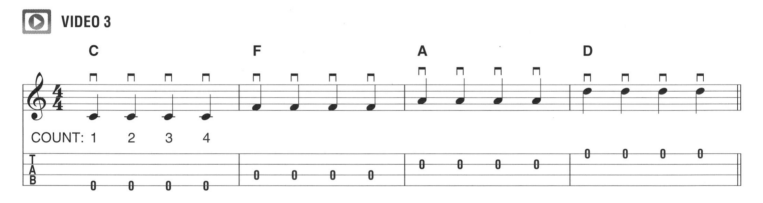

Now, try moving between courses:

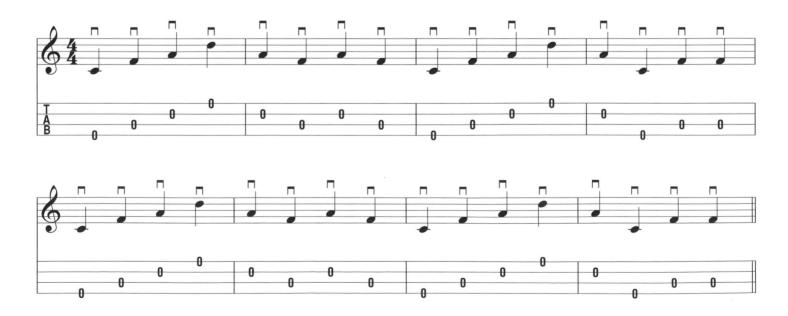

REPEATS

Repeat signs ‖:∶‖ show that the music in between them should be repeated. When you reach the repeat sign at the end of a section, return to the first sign and play the section again. Then proceed to the next section.

A pair of repeat signs means that you should play the music twice, unless you see a special instruction over the staff like "*play 3 times.*"

Now let's make it a little more interesting.

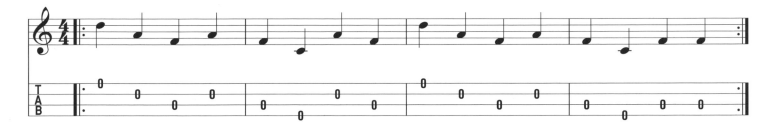

EIGHTH NOTES

A pair of **eighth notes** represents a quarter note split into two equal parts:

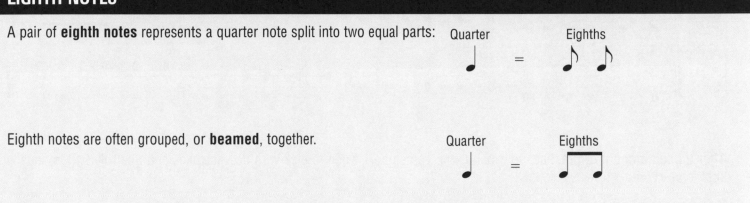

Eighth notes are often grouped, or **beamed**, together.

When you play eighth notes in sequence, the first note is played when your foot taps on the beat (the **downbeat**), and the second is played as your foot raises up (the **upbeat**). Two eighth notes take up one beat. You count the eighth notes as "one *and*, two *and*," etc.

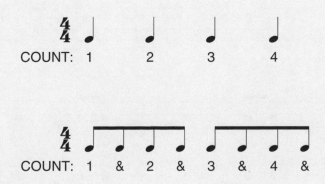

ALTERNATE PICKING

The most efficient way to play eighth notes is with **alternate picking**. This is a very important technique on the Greek bouzouki.

Pick the first note as a downstroke and the next note as an **upstroke**, as shown by this symbol: ⅴ Then alternate, playing with the same amount of force on each downstroke and upstroke.

▶ **VIDEO 4**

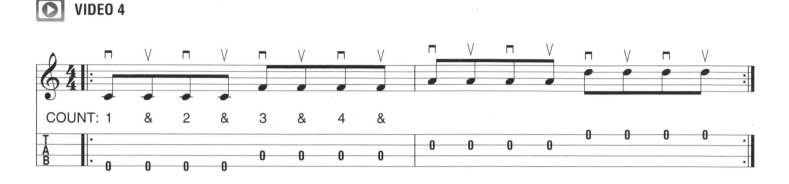

Now combine quarter and eighth notes. Watch the downstroke and upstroke symbols:

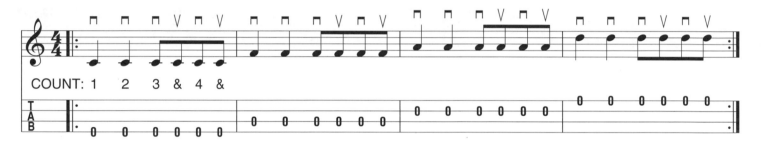

After a good amount of practice, your hand will "remember" when to pick with downstrokes and upstrokes. It is usually best to start with a downstroke.

▶ **VIDEO 5**

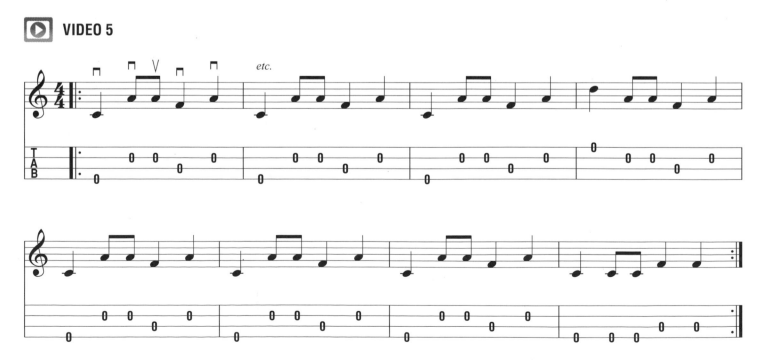

HALF NOTES

A **half note** takes up the space of two quarter notes. In 4/4 time, it sounds for two beats:

This example has two repeated sections!

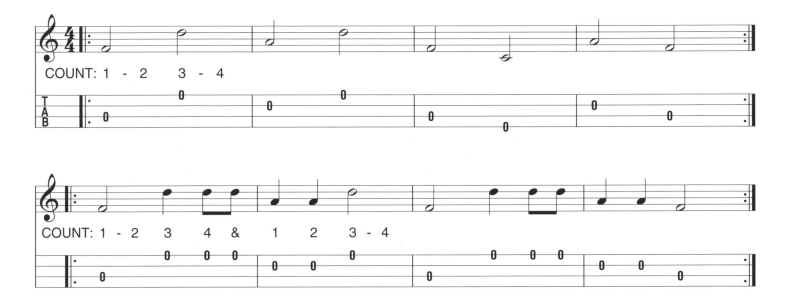

COUNT: 1 - 2   3 - 4

COUNT: 1 - 2   3   4   &   1   2   3 - 4

WHOLE NOTES

A **whole note** takes up a whole measure in 4/4 time. It sounds for four beats:

Play this one with all downstrokes.

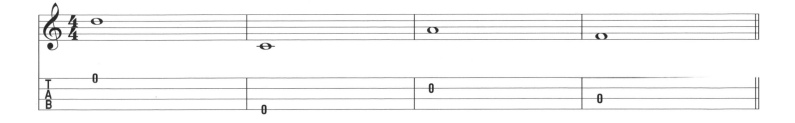

NOTES ON THE FIRST COURSE

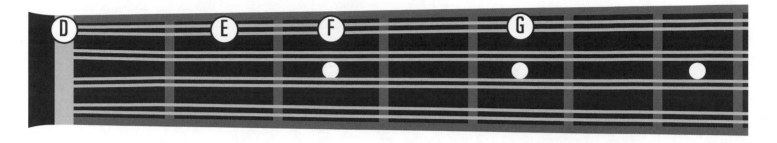

Left-hand fingerings are shown next to the notes.

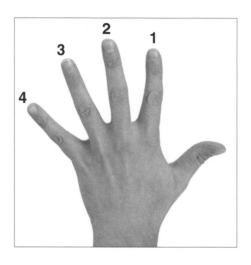

When you play **fretted notes**, press straight down on the strings *between* the metal frets. If you fret too softly or in the wrong place, the strings will buzz and sound unclear.

These examples feature open and fretted notes on the first string.

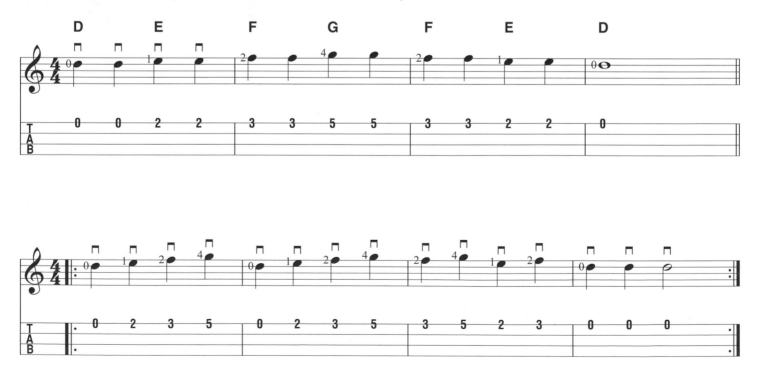

PRACTICE TIP: FRETTING

For good-sounding fretted notes, keep as many fingers on the fretboard as you can. In the previous examples, after you press on fret 2 with your first finger, keep that finger down when you add the second finger on fret 3. Keep both of those fingers down when you add your fourth finger on fret 5. Then simply pick up selective fingers when you go back down to frets 3 and 2. This will improve your speed and keep your hands healthy.

Now try some alternate picking and eighth notes.

  VIDEO 6

NOTES ON THE SECOND COURSE

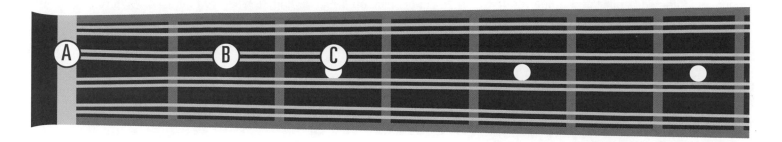

These examples will get you familiar with the basic notes on the second course. Take your time and run through each exercise multiple times until you can play the notes cleanly.

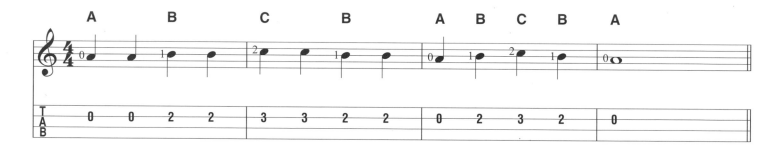

This one moves quickly between eighth notes. Try to pick all the notes evenly.

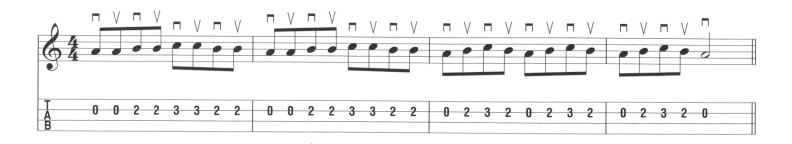

A **metronome** is a useful tool for developing technique. Mechanical, electronic, and app-based metronomes are easy to find from music stores or online. If an exercise is extra challenging, play it with a metronome at a very slow pace, then speed it up as you become more confident.

CROSSING STRINGS

Now you are ready to play some melodies on multiple string courses. Watch the downstroke and upstroke symbols and keep the alternate picking pattern going when you cross from one course to the next.

▶ VIDEO 7

Now try some eighth-note alternate picking.

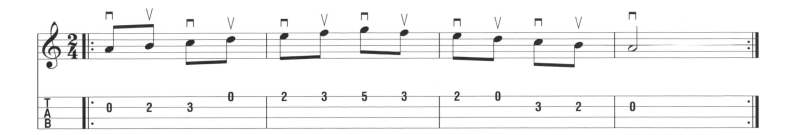

SLURS, HAMMER-ONS, AND PULL-OFFS

In the next example you will see a curved line connecting two different notes. This is a **slur**, indicating that the notes should flow smoothly together: Play the first note, then "hammer" your left-hand finger down on the second fret without picking. This is called a **hammer-on**.

The second measure begins with a **pull-off**. Pick the first note, then pull your left-hand finger downward off the fretboard without picking.

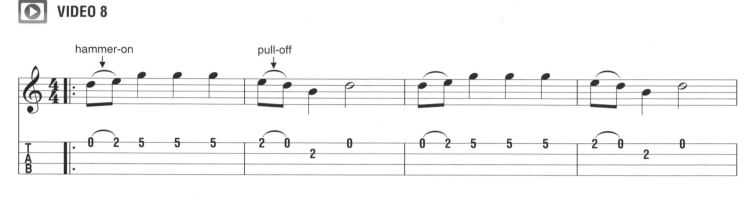

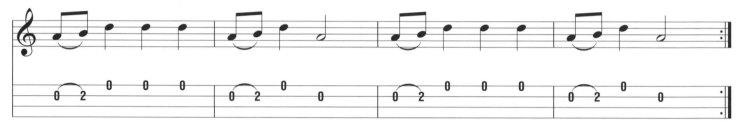

NOTES ON THE THIRD COURSE

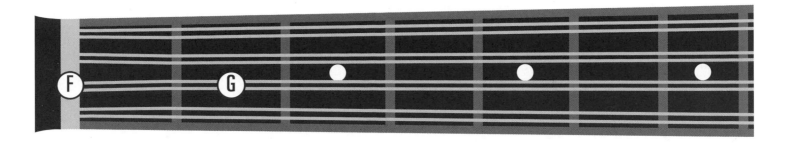

We are only looking at one fretted note on the third course for now, as it relates to the other strings in this position.

Here is an example that crosses between the third and second course:

Now try your hand at crossing between three strings.

BOUZOUKI FEVER

▶ VIDEO 10

♩ = 100

METRONOME MARKINGS

The symbol ♩ = 100 at the beginning of the song above indicates the tempo of the tune. 100 beats per minute (BPM) is the speed at which the tune is meant to be played, and each beat you hear represents one quarter note.

DOTTED NOTES

A **dot** after a note adds half of that note's value to it. In other words, the note sounds for one and a half times longer than it normally would. A **dotted half note** lasts the length of a half note plus a quarter note.

2 beats + 1 beat = 3 beats

"Ode to Joy" includes dotted quarter notes (lasting one and a half beats) and hammer-ons. Watch the video to hear and see the melody played over backing chords.

ODE TO JOY (MELODY)

Beethoven

VIDEO 11

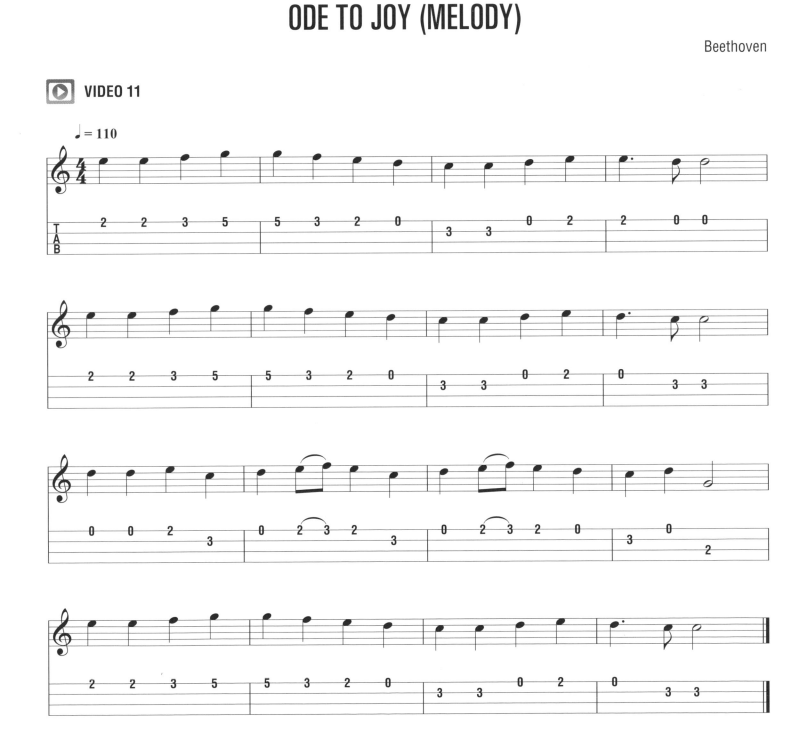

NOTES ON THE FOURTH COURSE

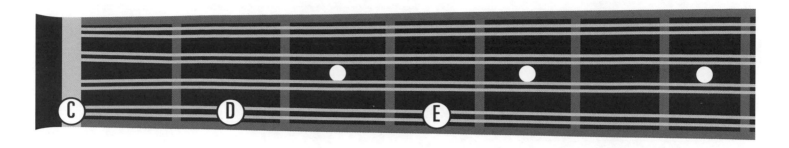

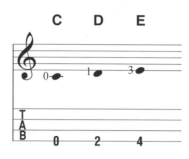

These examples will help you get familiar with the notes on the fourth course.

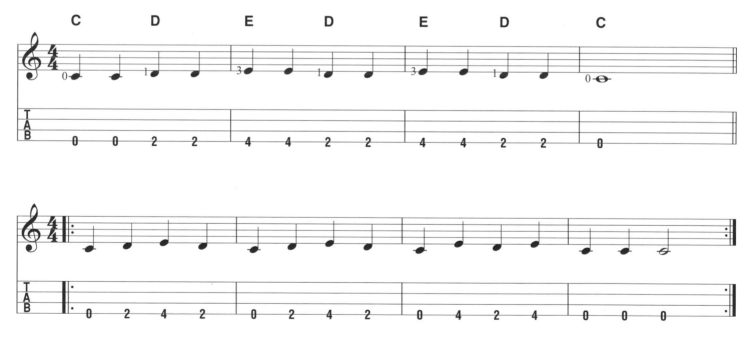

Now try it with eighth notes.

Now try crossing between the fourth and third strings, with a hammer-on:

Now cross between the fourth, third, and second strings:

AU CLAIR DE LA LUNE

French Folk Song

RESTS

For every note that lasts a certain amount of time, there is a **rest** of the same value that tells you how long *not* to play. Whenever you see a rest in music, stop playing and count the beat(s) of silence.

A **whole rest** is equal to four beats, or one measure in 4/4 time: ▬

A **half rest** is equal to two beats in 4/4 time: ▬

A **quarter rest** is equal to one beat in 4/4 and 2/4 time: 𝄽

An **eighth rest** is equal to one-half beat in 4/4 and 2/4 time: 𝄾

This example begins with a quarter rest. Count "1, 2, 3, 4, 1," then begin on beat 2.

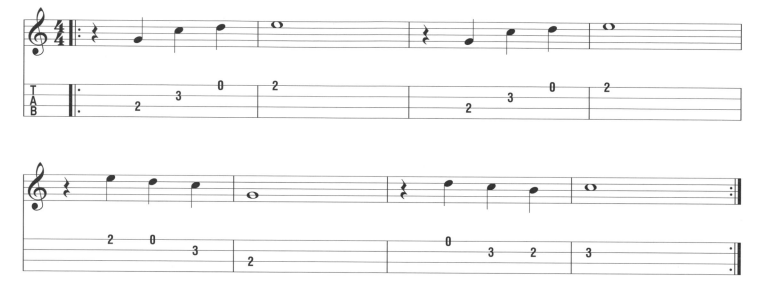

This song from the Greek island of Thessaly begins with a half rest followed by a quarter rest. Count "1, 2, 3," then begin on beat 4. Watch for dotted notes and slurs.

SYNTAZONTAI AVGERINES

Thessalian Folk Song

Finally, here is a tune that uses all four courses.

AEGEAN DREAM

▶ VIDEO 12

PRACTICE TIP

Want a fun challenge? Play through "Aegean Dream" again, this time letting the open strings ring out as long as possible. This will get you acquainted with the use of **drone strings**, which we will explore again soon.

C MAJOR SCALE

Everything you have played so far has used notes from the **C major scale**:

This is the C major scale in **open position**:

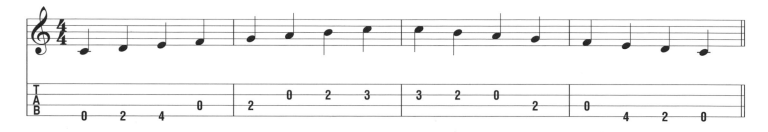

Now, using the rest of the notes you have learned, you can extend the C major scale:

PICKUP NOTES

Often, when a piece of music begins before beat 1, rather than writing out a complete measure with rests, we use **pickup notes**. The next tune begins with a quarter note leading into the first measure. Count "1, 2, 3," and begin on beat 4.

This classical melody jumps around the C major scale. Watch for slurs!

TROIKA

Prokofiev

▶ VIDEO 13

SECOND POSITION

We can extend scales over the entire range of the bouzouki by using different positions on the neck. Here is the C major scale in **second position**, anchored on fret 2:

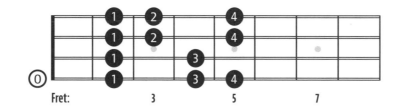

Here is a melody in second position. To play these three-note slurs, pick the first note, then hammer on and pull off.

THE AGORA

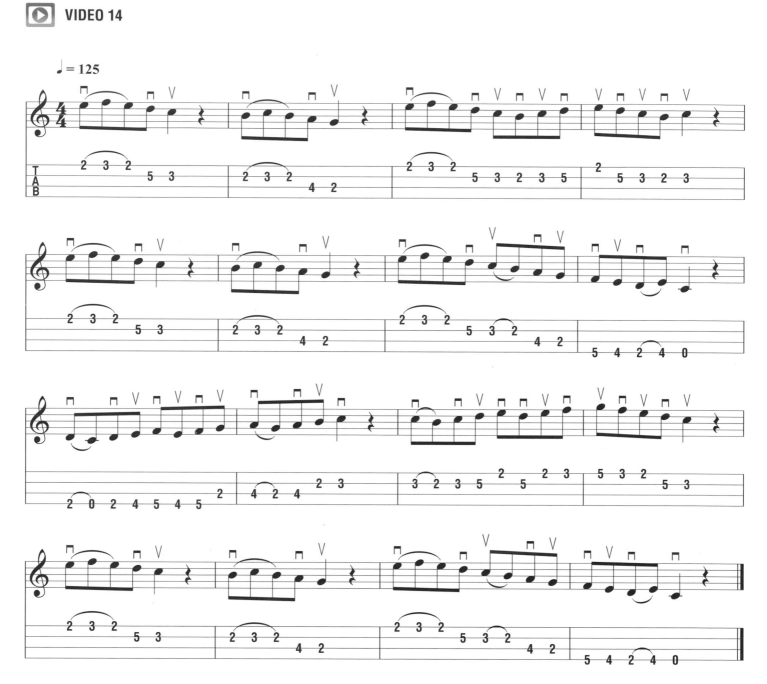

C, F, AND G CHORDS

Bouzoukists are mostly lead players, but we sometimes play chords (multiple notes played at the same time). Here are three chords in **open position** (with open strings as part of the chord).

These chord charts show where to put your fingers on the strings. An "X" means that string should not be played, and an "O" means an open string. Once your fingers are in position, strum all the strings in the chord at once.

C

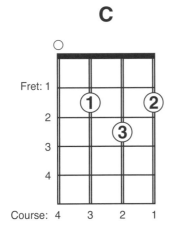

F

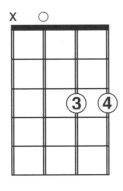

G

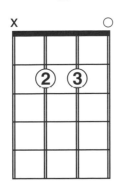

Remember playing "Ode to Joy" on the first, second, and third courses of strings? Here is a version with the accompanying chords. Strum the chords shown when their symbols appear above the measures. Use all downstrokes.

ODE TO JOY (CHORDS)

Beethoven

VIDEO 15

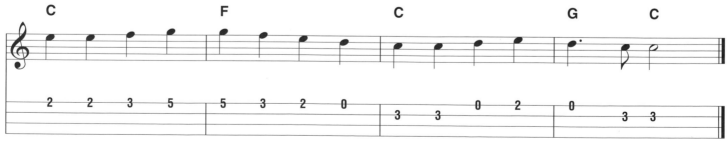

GRACE NOTES AND SLIDES

Greek bouzouki playing is distinguished by its use of **grace notes**, extra "mini-notes" added as decorations to the basic melody. Grace notes are often played as simple slurs:

...or as **slides**, by playing a note and sliding your finger up or down the fretboard to change the pitch. A slide is indicated with a slanted line and a slur:

This example has as a quick hammer-on from fret 2 to fret 3.

Watch the left-hand finger notation to see how your hand position will change with the slides in this example.

The same chords you learned for "Ode to Joy" can be used to play the accompaniment for "Divari." "N.C." above the staff means "no chord" and tells you to stop strumming the chords for that measure until the next chord name appears.

The melody includes a new note: a high A on the first course, fret 7. Watch the left-hand finger notation for position shifts.

DIVARI

▶ VIDEO 16

FIFTH POSITION

Here are the notes for the C major scale in **fifth position**, anchored at fret 5:

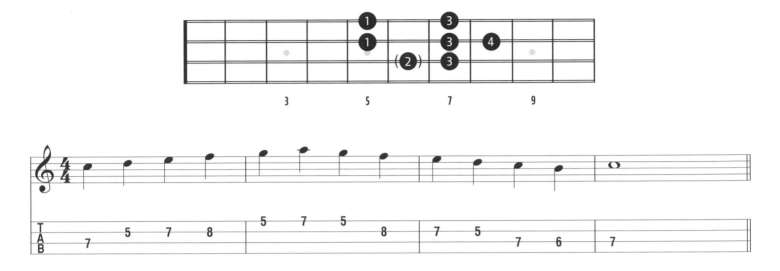

TIES

A **tie** is a curved line that connects two or more notes *of the same pitch* (unlike a slur, which connects two differently pitched notes). Tied notes are held, or sustained, for the combined length of the connected notes.

This example uses a **drone**, a single low note that sustains while the tune is played over it. The drone note is shown on the bottom of the staff, and the melody on top. Pick the open C course and let it ring while you play the melody in fifth position.

▶ **VIDEO 17**

ENDINGS

Sometimes a melody is repeated but does not end in exactly the same way the second time. We use first and second **endings** to distinguish between two variations of a melody.

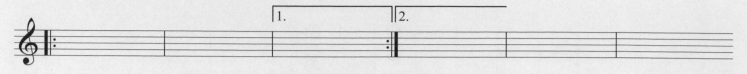

When you reach the repeat sign, return to the beginning of the section and play the part again. On the second time through, skip over the first ending (the bracketed measure labeled with a "1"), go to the second ending, and play on to the end.

BOUZOUKI TIME!

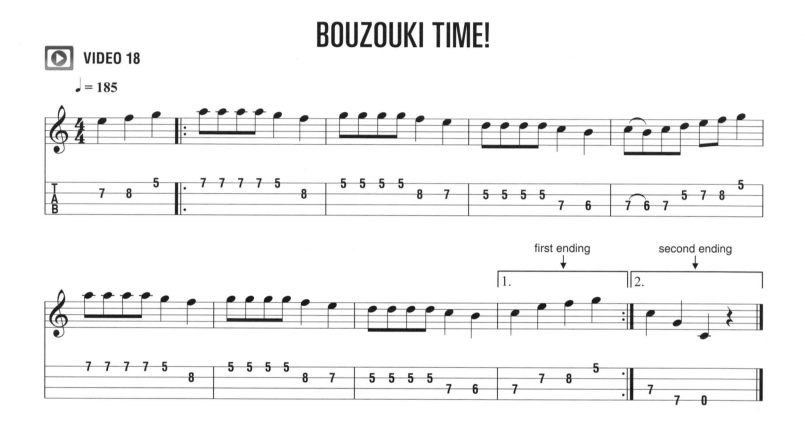

THE BOUZOUKI FAMILY

The *tetrachordo* bouzouki is part of an extended family that includes its smaller three-course cousins:

- the *baglamas*, a tiny three-course bouzouki that plays high, chimey chords;

- the *tsouras*, a medium-sized 'zouk that also covers upper melodies and rhythm;

- the more traditional-style *trichordo* bouzouki.

SEVENTH POSITION

Here are the notes for the C major scale in **seventh position**:

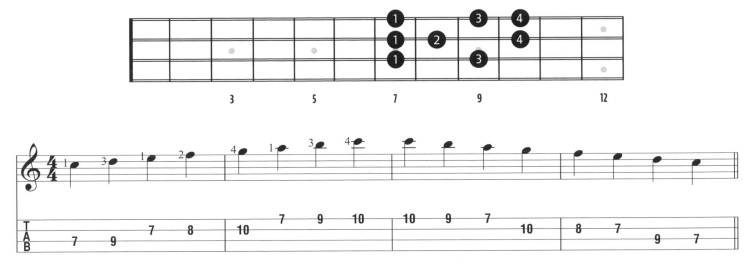

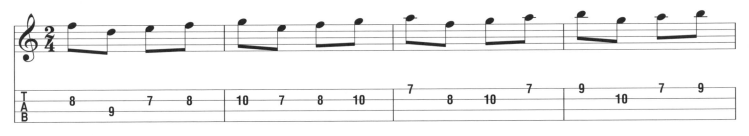

Here is an exercise to get you familiar with the position:

Now you are ready to cross between the seventh, fifth, second, and open positions.

▶ **VIDEO 19**

NINTH POSITION

The next tune introduces a new "mini-position" of the C major scale anchored at fret 9.

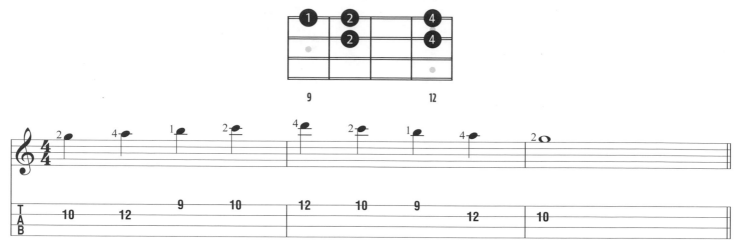

"Gelmeden" shifts between ninth and seventh positions. The **fermata** symbol (⌢) at the end means that the last note should be held beyond the usual length of the measure.

GELMEDEN

▶ VIDEO 20

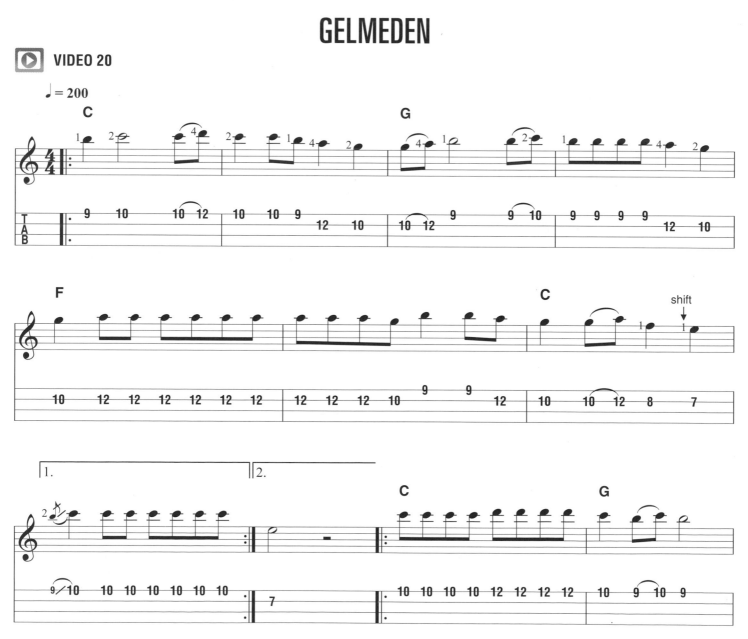

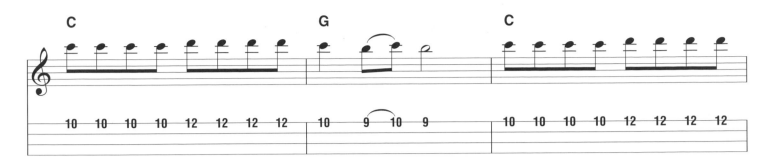

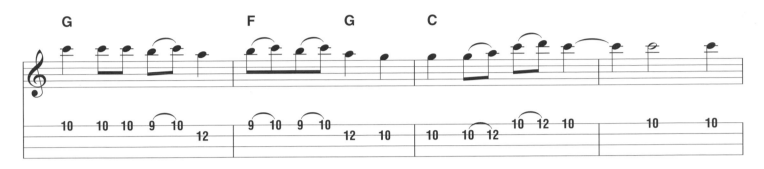

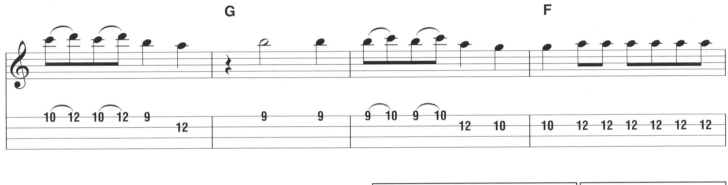

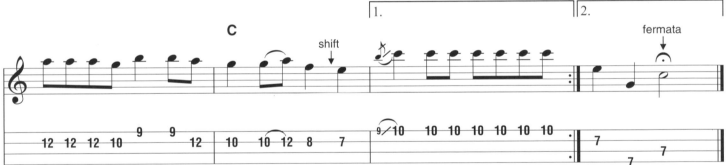

SHARPS AND FLATS

A **sharp** sign (♯) next to a note raises it by one half step, or one fret. A **flat** sign (♭) shows that the note is lowered by one half step. A **natural** sign (♮) cancels out a previous sharp or flat note. Collectively, these signs are called **accidentals**.

Flats and sharps are usually interchangeable—a B♭ is the same as an A♯—but which sign you use often depends on the **key signature**, which you will learn soon.

CHROMATIC NOTES

The **chromatic scale** is made up of all half steps. In other words, it contains all the notes you can play on the bouzouki. Here is the chromatic scale in open position:

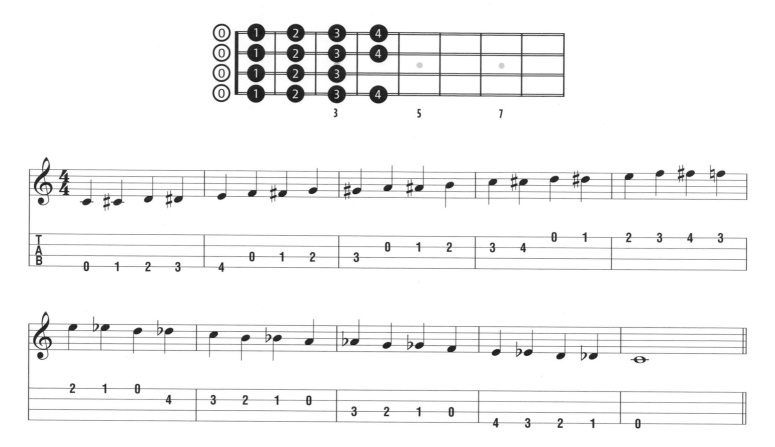

Greek music often uses chromatic notes within melodies. Play the following examples to get a feel for where chromatic notes are effective.

Once a note is marked sharp or flat, it remains so for the rest of the measure it appears in, unless you see a natural sign to cancel it. The F note in this example is marked as an F♯ until the fifth full measure, where it is played as F natural. (It doesn't require a natural sign because there is no F♯ in the measure to cancel.) Sometimes, as a helpful reminder, there will be a **courtesy accidental** shown in the measure after an accidental is used.

STACCATO

A dot placed over or under a notehead means that it should be played **staccato**, or short. Play the note, then **mute** it slightly by taking your left-hand finger off the fretboard (but not off the string). You can also use your right hand to dampen the string right after you pluck it.

This kind of **riff**, or repeating phrase, is often used in bellydance-style music. Pay attention to the sharps and naturals in the notation.

VIDEO 21

SHUFFLE

In **shuffle** or **swing feel**, each pair of eighth notes is played as a long note followed by a short note, more like a heartbeat than a regular beat. It is indicated at the top of the music with this symbol:

Greek music makes great use of this, often playing "straight" eighth notes against a shuffle feel.

VIDEO 22

Triplets are groups of three notes that fit evenly into the space that would usually be taken up by two of the same kind of note. An **eighth-note triplet** takes up the space of two regular eighth notes, or one quarter note:

A MINOR CHORD

The following example ends with a new chord: A minor. Here is what it looks like on the neck and in notation:

Am

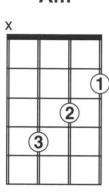

This is a **closed-position** chord; it has no open strings. When you know a few closed-position chord shapes, you can play many different chords all over the neck.

This popular folk melody uses staccato chromatic notes and triplets with an eighth-note swing feel.

VIDEO 23

HARMONY

Traditional Greek music is often played in groups that include multiple bouzoukis, a *baglamas* and/or *tsouras*, and rhythm guitar or *lauto* (Greek lute). A pair of bouzoukis playing harmony parts is characteristic in these ensembles.

When two bouzoukis **harmonize**, they often play in **thirds**. For example, when one bouzouki plays a C note, the other plays an E, which is the third note of the C major scale. We notate them with connected staves:

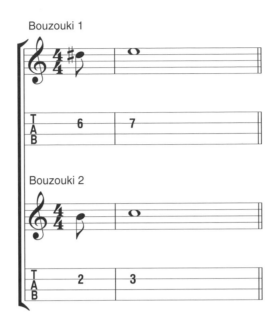

3/4 TIME

In a **3/4** time signature, there are three beats per measure, and a quarter note gets one beat. You might recognize it as a "waltz" feel.

COUNT: 1 - 2 - 3 | 1 - 2 - 3 | 1 - 2 - 3

D.S. AL FINE

In a piece of music with many repeats, we use special repeat instructions to guide the player. **D.S. al Fine**, or *Dal Segno al Fine*, means "from the sign to the end." When you see this instruction, go back to the sign 𝄋, and play on to the measure marked **Fine**, the end.

"The Olive Grove" has three parts you can learn: the main melody (Bouzouki 1), the harmony part (Bouzouki 2), and the chords.

THE OLIVE GROVE

VIDEO 24 – BOUZOUKI 1

VIDEO 25 – BOUZOUKI 2

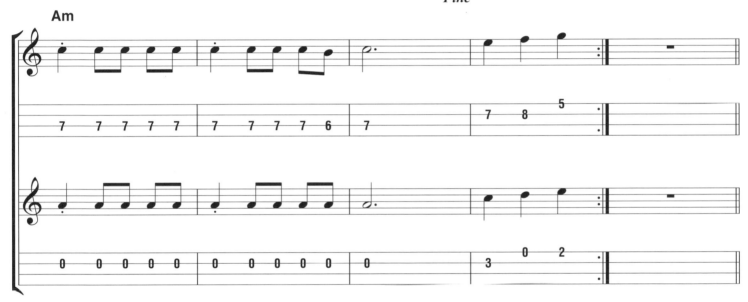

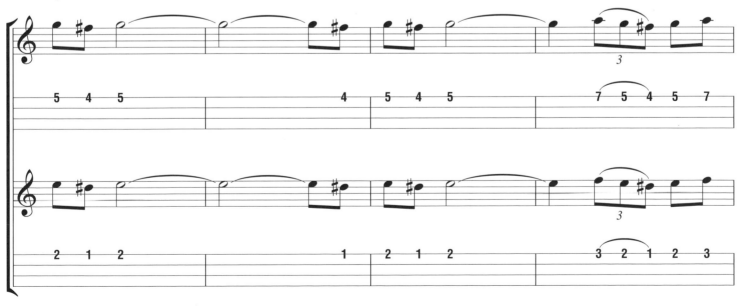

G

D.S. al Fine

A MINOR SCALE

The notes of the **A minor scale** are the same as the C major scale, with different starting and ending points. We call A minor the **relative minor** of C major.

Here are two positions of the A minor scale, anchored on the second and seventh fret.

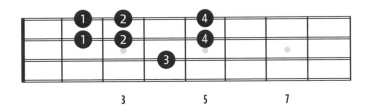

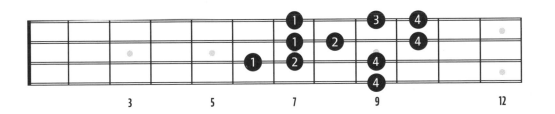

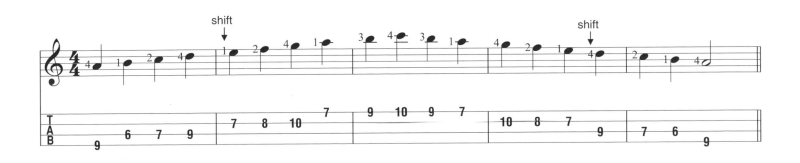

SNAKE CHARMER

▶ VIDEO 26

SIXTEENTH NOTES

Sixteenth notes represent a quarter note split into four equal parts:

These four sixteenth notes beamed together equal one beat:

This grouping of notes is played with one eighth note on the downbeat and two sixteenth notes on the upbeat:

A MINOR BARRE CHORD

The following song ends with a new voicing of the A minor chord. To play this closed-position chord shape, lay your first finger flat over the first, second, and third courses, and fret the fourth course at fret 9 with your third finger. This is called a **barre chord**.

Am

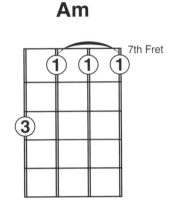

"Mermaid" begins with a pair of sixteenth pickup notes. Count "one, and-a, two, and-a, three, and-a, four," and start playing on "and-a."

MERMAID

VIDEO 27

MORE CHORDS

Closed-position major and minor chords come in a few varieties that can be used all over the neck. You have already used two closed-position shapes for A minor. Here are two major chord shapes:

This E chord is a barre, with the first finger covering the first two strings:

This A chord is like a closed version of the open G chord:

E

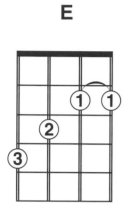

A

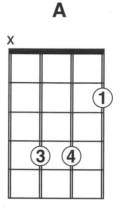

Now you are ready to integrate chords and melodies. In this example, the chord symbols are there to show where to position your left hand on the fretboard. Use the E major chord shape on fret 5 to play the G chord, then move it to fret 3 to play the F chord.

▶ VIDEO 28

ARPEGGIOS

When you play the notes of a chord one at a time, upward or downward, you create an **arpeggio**. This tune is built on **arpeggiated** E major and A minor chords. It also gives you some practice playing repeated sixteenth notes.

TSIFTETELI

VIDEO 29

D HARMONIC MINOR SCALE

Here is a scale that crosses the boundaries between major and minor. The **harmonic minor scale** is like a minor scale with a major seventh note. Below are two positions of the D harmonic minor scale.

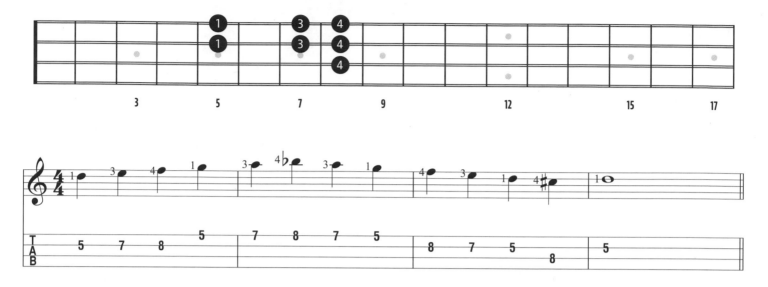

This position has different fingerings while ascending and descending, as shown in the staff below.

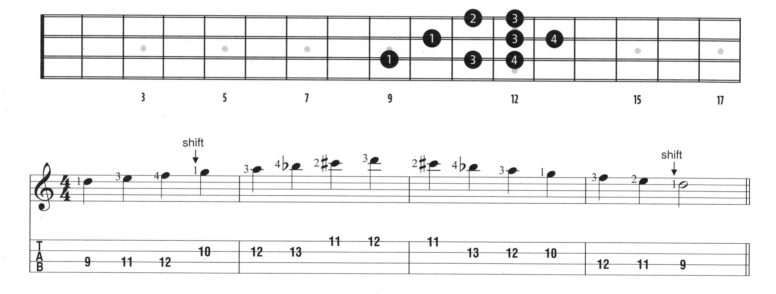

KEY SIGNATURES

Instead of writing a flat sign before every B in a tune, one flat is shown at the beginning of the staff. This is called a **key signature**. This one, for the key of D minor, indicates that every B in the music should be played as B♭.

"Apo Tin Athina" is the Greek version of a song that is popular in many Balkan and Mediterranean countries. The ascending melody can be considered a D minor scale with a C♮ note; it goes into harmonic minor with a C# when it descends.

APO TIN ATHINA

9/8 TIME

The **9/8** time signature is very popular in bouzouki music, especially the *Rebetiko* style of urban Greek folk that flourished in the first half of the 20th century and continues to be popular today.

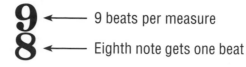

9 ← 9 beats per measure

8 ← Eighth note gets one beat

A common kind of 9/8 pattern is known in Greece as *Zeibekiko Kamilieriko*. A good way to count it is to **subdivide** it into smaller beat groups:

COUNT:	1	-	2	1	-	2	1	-	2	1	-	2	-	3
BEAT:	1		2	3		4	5		6	7		8		9

This slow 9/8 folk song begins with pickup notes. Count "1–2, 1–2, 1–2," and start playing on beat 7. Note the F# in the key signature—play every F as an F#.

ANDILALOUN I FYLAKES

▶ **VIDEO 31**

THIRTY-SECOND NOTES

A sixteenth note can be split into two **thirty-second notes**:

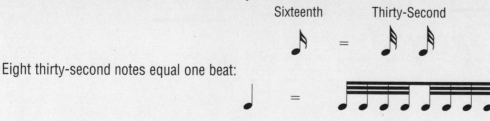

Sixteenth   Thirty-Second

Eight thirty-second notes equal one beat:

In a slow 9/8 pattern, thirty-second notes are not played as fast as you might think! The Rebetiko classic on the next page is in D harmonic minor with extra chromatic notes, grace notes, and staccato notes, plus hammer-ons and pull-offs.

D.C. (or *Da Capo*) means "from the head (beginning)." After taking all repeats, go back to the top of the song and play (with repeats again) until you reach the final measure.

TO MINORE TOU TEKE

Traditional

♪ = 93

D.C.
(take repeats)

D HIJAZ MODE

A **mode**, like a scale, is a series of notes arranged in a sequence of rising and falling pitches. Unlike most scales, modes do not always correspond to standard major and minor keys. **Hijaz** (a.k.a. *Hitzaz* or *Hicaz*) is one such mode.

Because of its unusual arrangement on the neck, playing in Hijaz involves a lot of position shifting. Here is one basic fingering, subject to change depending on the melody you are playing:

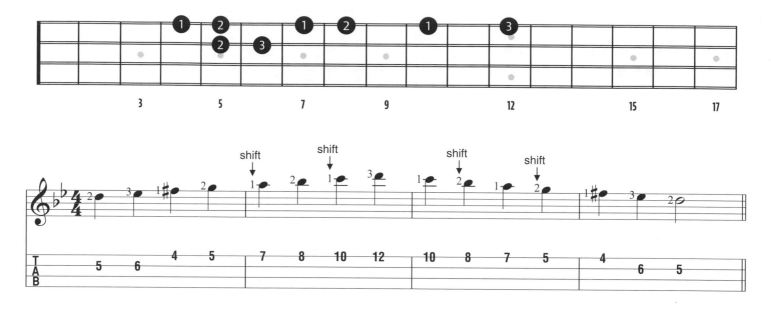

"Hasaposerviko" will give you some good position-shifting practice in Hijaz mode. The fingering changes according to the position shifts.

HASAPOSERVIKO

▶ **VIDEO 33**

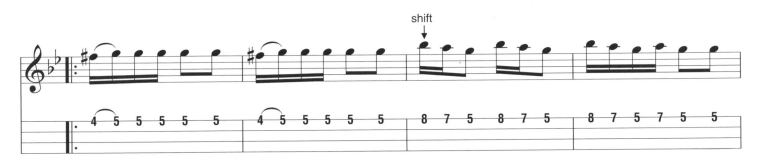

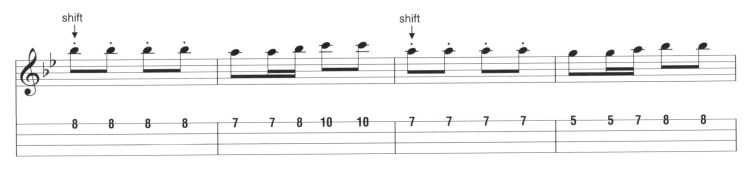

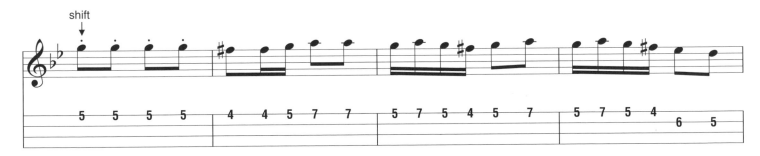

HIJAZ KAR

Hijaz Kar is a variation of Hijaz mode with a major seventh note. Here is one fingering for it in D (again, subject to change):

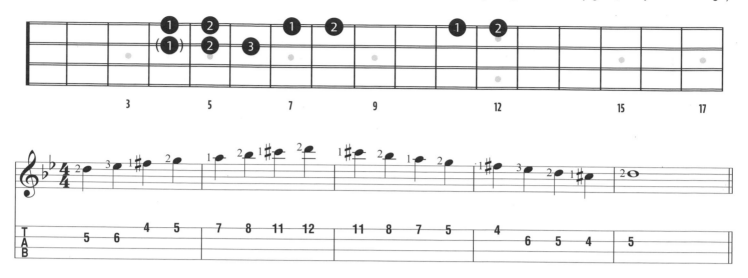

PLAYING BEYOND THE TWELFTH FRET

When you reach the twelfth fret on the bouzouki, everything repeats an octave higher. For example, an open C note on the fourth course is a higher C note on fret 12. That means everything you play below fret 12 can be played an octave higher—just go twelve frets up!

Here is a position of Hijaz Kar in the higher range. Notice that the notes are in the same place on the staff even though they sound higher. The symbol **8va** tells you to play those notes an octave higher than written, while the tab staff still shows the actual neck position. This is simply a way to keep the notes easier to read on the staff.

"Danse Bacchanale" from Camille Saint-Saens' *Samson and Delilah* is one of very few European classical pieces to use Hijaz Kar (also known as **double harmonic major**). Play the melody once through, then repeat an octave up as shown.

DANSE BACCHANALE (EXCERPT)

Saint-Saens

▶ VIDEO 34

MORE ABOUT MODES

The **modes of the major scale** were developed in the Middle Ages based on ancient Greek treatises. They contain all the notes of a major scale, in different sequences and different keys. There are also many modes from Mediterranean and Middle Eastern traditions that do not fit into the major-scale mode system, like Hijaz and Hijaz Kar.

E OUSSAK MODE

One of the modes that does fit into the major-scale mode system is **Oussak** (a.k.a **Phrygian mode**). E Oussak mode is the third mode of C major; you can play it using many of the same scale positions you learned for C major! Here is Oussak mode in second and seventh position:

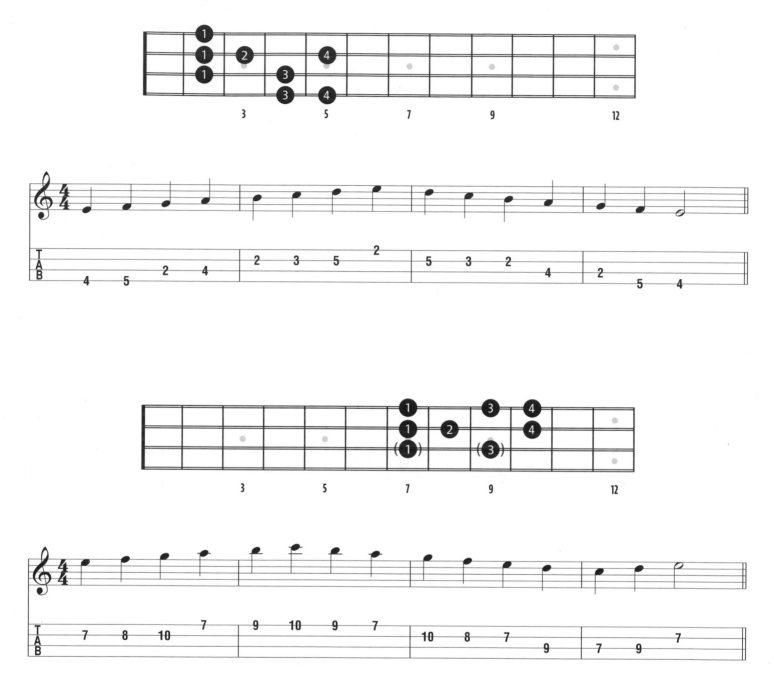

Compare this to the C major scale in second and seventh position (pages 27 and 33); it is the same scale with different starting and ending notes.

KANE KOURAGIO

7/8 TIME

The **7/8** time signature is also very popular in Greek music and dance.

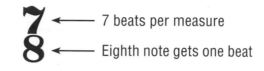

7 → 7 beats per measure

8 → Eighth note gets one beat

In *Kalamatiano* rhythm, a measure of 7/8 is subdivided into three parts:

COUNT: 1 - 2 - 3   1 - 2   1 - 2
BEAT: 1   2   3   4   5   6   7

"I Mana Mou Me Derni" begins with three pickup notes. When counting in, give yourself an extra measure of 7/8. Count "1–2–3, 1–2, 1–2, 1–2–3, 1," and start playing.

I MANA MOU ME DERNI (INTRO)

Traditional

▶ VIDEO 36

SPECIAL TECHNIQUES

TREMOLO PICKING

A signature technique of bouzouki music is **tremolo picking**, which involves rapidly alternating downstrokes and upstrokes. You have already played alternating sixteenth and thirty-second notes; tremolo picking is like a high-speed version of the same technique. To develop steady tremolo technique, start with eighth notes, work up to sixteenths, then thirty-seconds.

Tremolo is indicated in notation with **slashes**, like this:

GRACE-NOTE TRILLS

You have already played some **trills** using quick hammer-ons and pull-offs. Bouzoukists use a distinctive grace-note trill that involves short, quick, repeated hammer-ons. Pick, hammer on, then quickly mute to create a staccato note:

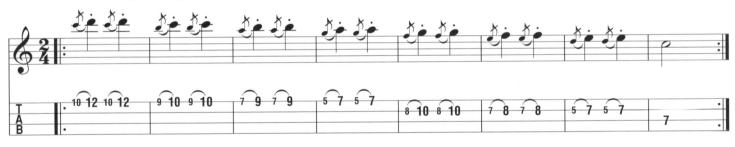

STACCATO WALTZ

▶ VIDEO 37

♩ = 180

DOUBLE STOPS

As a solo bouzoukist, you can harmonize with yourself using **double stops**. These are two-note mini-chords, usually played on string pairs 1 and 2, or 2 and 3. With a few basic shapes, you can play double stops all over the neck.

Here is the **D major scale** outlined in double stops:

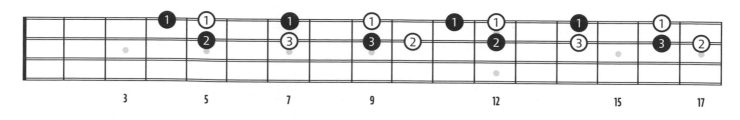

Again, these fingerings are not strict—they can change according to where the shapes fall in the music.

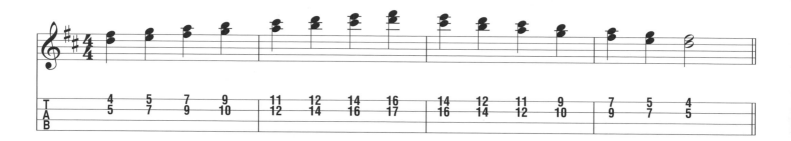

Double stops are often played with tremolo picking. Pick cleanly so that both notes ring at an equal volume.

BOUZOUKI LULLABYE

▶ VIDEO 38

Here is a swinging tune that uses all the special techniques: grace-note trills, staccato notes, triplets, slides, and tremolo-picked double stops. Opa!

NYCHTO POULI

VIDEO 39

RESOURCES

Here are some useful tools to refer to as you continue your adventures as a bouzoukist. Yassou!

NOTES ON THE FRETBOARD

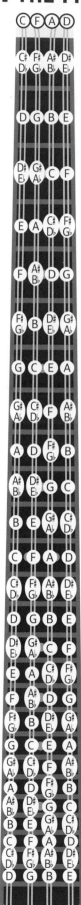

CHORD SHAPES

These are the most common closed positions used for major and minor chords. For each chord shape, the **root note** (note on which the chord is based) is circled. To play a C major chord, find a C note on the fretboard, and use the chord shape shown with that note as the root:

C Major

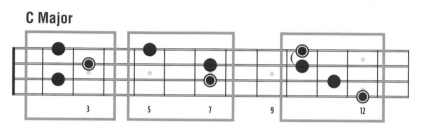

MAJOR CHORDS	MINOR CHORDS

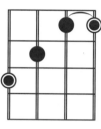

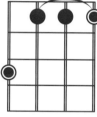

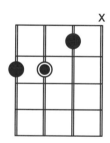

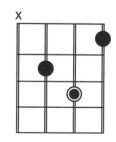

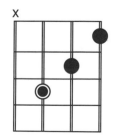